Clouds

by Gail Saunders-Smith

Content Consultant:
Ken Barlow, Chief Meteorologist
KARE-TV, Minneapolis
Member, American Meteorological Society

Pebble Books
an Imprint of Capstone Press

Pebble Books

Pebble Books are published by Capstone Press
818 North Willow Street, Mankato, Minnesota 56001
http://www.capstone-press.com

Library of Congress Cataloging-in-Publication Data
Saunders-Smith, Gail.
    Clouds/by Gail Saunders-Smith.
        p. cm.
    Includes bibliographical references and index.
    Summary: Describes different kinds of clouds—cirrus, cumulus, stratus, and nimbus—
and the types of weather they indicate.
    ISBN 1-56065-777-4
    1. Clouds—Juvenile literature. [1. Clouds.] I. Title.
    QC921.35.S28 1998
    551.57′6—dc21   98-5051
                                                                         CIP
                                                                          AC

Note to Parents and Teachers

This book describes and illustrates many kinds of clouds and the type of
weather they indicate. The close picture-text matches support early readers in
understanding the text. The text offers subtle challenges with compound and
complex sentence structures. This book also introduces early readers to
expository and content-specific vocabulary. The expository vocabulary is
defined in the Words to Know section. Early readers may need assistance in
reading some of these words. Readers also may need assistance in using the
Table of Contents, Words to Know, Read More, Internet Sites, and Index/Word
List sections of the book.

452-3949

Table of Contents

What Clouds Are 5
Kinds of Clouds 9

Note to Parents and Teachers 2
Words to Know 22
Read More 23
Internet Sites 23
Index/Word List 24

Clouds form when warm air rises and cools. Clouds are made of very small water drops. The drops stick to dust in the air.

Clouds bring rain and snow. Rain falls when the air is above the freezing temperature. Snow falls when the air is below the freezing temperature.

Clouds come in many shapes. Meteorologists study cloud shapes. A meteorologist is a person who studies the weather. The shapes of the clouds tell meteorologists what kind of weather is coming.

Cirrus clouds form high in the sky. They are very thin. People can see through cirrus clouds. Cirrus clouds mean that it will rain or snow within 24 hours.

Cumulus clouds have flat bottoms and puffy tops. Small, white cumulus clouds mean good weather. Big, dark cumulus clouds bring thunder and heavy rain.

14

Stratus clouds are gray and flat. They cover most of the sky. They form low in the sky. Light snow or drizzle sometimes falls from stratus clouds. Drizzle is a light rain.

Nimbostratus clouds are like stratus clouds. They are flat and cover most of the sky. But they are dark gray. They form higher in the sky. Nimbostratus clouds bring rain or snow.

Fog is a cloud, too. Fog happens when a cloud forms close to the ground. Fog goes away when the water drops dry up. Wind and heat can make fog dry up.

Clouds carry rain and snow. Wind pushes clouds across the sky. Clouds carry water to places all over the world.

Words to Know

cirrus—thin clouds that form high in the sky

cumulus—clouds with flat bottoms and high, puffy tops

drizzle—a light rain

dust—tiny pieces of dirt that gather in the air

flat—something that does not have dips or bumps

freezing—very cold; the point at which water turns to ice, which is 32 degrees Fahrenheit (0 degrees Celsius)

meteorologist—a person who studies the weather

nimbostratus—flat, dark gray clouds that cover most of the sky; nimbostratus clouds are like stratus clouds, but they form higher in the sky

puffy—when something looks soft, light, and filled with air

stratus—flat, gray clouds that cover most of the sky

temperature—the measure of how hot or cold something is

Read More

Berger, Melvin and Gilda Berger. *How's the Weather.* Nashville, Tenn.: Ideals Children's Books, 1993.

Fowler, Allan. *What Do You See in a Cloud?* New York: Children's Press, 1996.

Merk, Ann. *Clouds.* Vero Beach, Fl.: Rourke Corp., 1994.

Supraner, Robyn. *I Can Read about the Weather.* Mahwah, N.J.: Troll, 1997.

Internet Sites

Athena, Earth and Space Science for K-12
http://Inspire.ospi.wednet.edu:8001/index.html

Dan's Wild Wild Weather Page
http://www.whnt19.com/kidwx/index.html

UIUC Cloud Catalog
http://covis.atmos.uiuc.edu/guide/clouds/html/oldhome.html

Index/Word List

air, 5, 7
bottoms, 13
cirrus clouds, 11
clouds, 5, 7, 9, 11, 13, 15, 17, 19, 21
cumulus clouds, 13
drizzle, 15
drops, 5, 19
dust, 5
fog, 19
ground, 19
heat, 19

meteorologist, 9
nimbostratus clouds, 17
people, 11
person, 9
places, 21
rain, 7, 11, 13, 15, 17, 21
shapes, 9
sky, 11, 15, 17, 21
snow, 7, 11, 15, 17, 21

stratus clouds, 15, 17
temperature, 7
thunder, 13
tops, 13
water, 5, 19, 21
weather, 9, 13
wind, 19, 21
world, 21

Word Count: 249
Early-Intervention Level: 10

Editorial Credits
Lois Wallentine, editor; Timothy Halldin, design; Michelle L. Norstad, photo research

Photo Credits
Cheryl A. Ertlet, 1, 16
PictureSmith/Larry Mishkar, cover
Cheryl R. Richter, 4, 14, 20
Root Resources/John Kohont, 6, 18; Louise K. Broman, 10
Unicorn Stock Photos/Jim Shippee, 8
Brian A. Vikander, 12